Becoming Me After You

Blending Memories of the Past with Hopes for the Future

Mary Jane Cronin LMHC
Wiggle Bug Publishing

© 2021 Mary Jane Cronin

ISBN: 978-0-9845016-7-0

Publisher's Note

This publication is designed to provide accurate and authoritative information in regard to the subject matter covered.

The suggestions and information gathered in this book are not designed to replace treatment. Contact a local physician or a counselor if desiring treatment.

Dedication

To the most important people in my life, my sons Jaime, Jesse, and Jonathan who have supported and encouraged me in my desire to help others with their loss and grief. To my guardian angel Jeremy who has guided me from heaven to continue my mission of helping others.

Acknowledgments

I wish to thank the brave men and women who shared their stories of loss with me. I have discovered that re-telling our story of grief ensures that our loved ones remain in our hearts. In taking the lessons we have learned from them; we are able to blossom, grow and thrive in their memories.

Thank you to Robin Powell for her talent in editing my book several times as we worked together in its creation.

A book may be filled with useful and enjoyable words, but the cover is the first thing that catches our eyes. I wish to thank Scott Howard for his patience, talent and creativity in making my cover shine.

Contents

"If there comes a day when we can't be together, keep

me in your heart, I'll stay there forever"

Winnie the Pooh

Preface

My personal loss history began before I can remember. When I was eight months old my twin brother and I were removed from a neglectful household and placed with a foster family.

Fostering turned into adoption as I held onto the hand of my "new" dad hoping the judge would see this was where I belonged. He agreed and I remained with them until I was an adult.

Unlike many of my older natural siblings who were placed in foster care, I had no loss connected to the event, except maybe the feeling that I knew I wasn't wanted and later feeling like I didn't belong.

As a child growing up in my new family I experienced the natural deaths of grandparents, aunts and uncles. Learning that death is a natural part of life I was sad and mourned their departure but accepted the death easily.

When my dad died, however, I discovered there was a deeper sense of loss, a deeper level of sadness.

Twenty years of calling him dad, of spending time talking about everything, and having him walk me down the aisle to give me away, I never thought about the day he would be taken away from me.

Anyone who has become a mother or father can understand the intensity of love felt the minute you held that child in your arms.

Sadly, the intensity of that love turned to an equally intense grief following the death of my son in 1998. Away from my extended family and without coping skills to deal with such a catastrophic loss, I retreated inward. While I sobbed alone in my bed thinking I was protecting his brothers from becoming upset or to see me upset, I was only teaching them to suppress their feelings.

I thought if I stuffed those feelings inside, they would go away. I know now that to begin healing you need to be open to the presence of your loss.

You need to begin to understand that it is not important to have all the "whys" answered, for that will not bring them back to you or help you find a resolution.

What I have learned over the years is that we heal from our hearts not from our brains. All the intellectual information we are given will not help us feel better or soothe our aching heart.

Mourning is not seen as a competition or race. There is no prize for speed. For years I would try to convince others that losing my son was

somehow more devastating a loss than theirs. What I came to understand is that everyone's loss is unique to them and is the most important.

None of us are free from losses in our life. Some will be simple like my grandparents and we will remember, mourn, and continue to live life as we know it. Other losses, the major ones, like my father and my son and possibly your loved one, can tear us to the core of our heart and can take a little more time, care and intervention.

It is important to listen to those who care, to those who support your loss and want to help you on your journey. Healing begins with your heart, not with your head. I wrote this book because I care and I am here to help you through your loss.

Mary Jane

Introduction to the Members

Eight strangers sat quietly around a table. They had come from diverse backgrounds and it was the first time they had met each other. Strangers, each one with their own personal story, but all had something in common. Each had experienced a special loss in their lives and needed support finding their way back home, back from the pain.

Two of the women had recently lost their mothers, three had lost their spouses and one had lost their lifelong pet. Two men had also enrolled in the group, an elderly man who had lost his wife and another had experienced the death of his adult son.

They'd all heard about the group and how it could help them work through the loss and the emptiness they were feeling. Choosing this particular group, they were each looking for a way to release their pain, honor their loved one, and learn a way to carry those memories into the future.

As they started talking to each other they shared a little bit about their own stories and what brought them to the group.

Cathy, one of the women, looked around and slowly started to talk. "It's been about six months since I lost my mom. She was living in a memory care unit and I visited her daily and spent hours with her.

Sometimes I visited even more than one time a day. It was pretty much my whole life, and now I feel empty.

Before she moved into the assisted living, she had been living in her own condo".

"Hiring a home health care agency was a gift to me because they gave me some much-needed breaks. Daily visits from the agency were helpful but mom kept calling on the telephone asking me to come over. As her primary caregiver, I found I still had to visit her daily, something I regretfully wished I didn't have to do".

I would do all the cooking and cleaning myself because my siblings had moved much farther away and had responsibilities that prevented them from helping, or so they all said.

We did not have a close mother-daughter relationship most of my life. She worked the majority of my school years and us kids were left home alone after school to do homework and fix ourselves dinner.

I married and moved away to a town a few miles away as soon as I finished high school. We still kept in touch but it was a distant relationship".

"When it was discovered that she could not manage her own care needs, I drove to her home often to help her. Convinced she could care for herself, she resented my intervention and our visits often ended with her being exhausted and going to lay down, and me driving home in tears, exhausted and needing to lay down myself".

Cathy said as her mother's decline increased, they were able to mend their relationship. "We talked and hugged as she told me she was sorry for pushing me away so often in my childhood and as an adult". "Her death left me wishing we had more time together to continue mending our broken relationship".

Judy had been her husband's caregiver for over ten years.

She had been working as a secretary at a bank when his health began to decline. It seemed that most of her time now was spent providing for his care and meeting his needs. She said at her age doing this often left her feeling drained.

Judy said her husband had Parkinson's disease and it had been a real struggle keeping him home. She took a drink of water and told them her story.

More than 50 years ago, she had married the love of her life, Bob. They started a family and built a wonderful life together in Maine then retired in Florida. Bob loved to dabble in painting scenic murals and landscapes in his spare time.

Things had been going wonderfully for them, but about ten years ago, she began to notice that he wasn't himself. His hands would shake, and he had trouble concentrating on the artwork.

"It was shortly after that that Bob was diagnosed with Parkinson's disease. A moment in time that changed our lives and altered the course of our future together forever".

Bob was not one to give up without a fight, and continued to search for educational or therapeutic programs to stay active and keep his illness from escalating.

One of the programs they found that helped was called Rock Steady Boxing, a nonprofit organization with centers in every state of the USA. Through exercises and various programs, it gives people with Parkinson's disease hope by improving their quality of life through a non-contact boxing-based fitness curriculum.

Not only did it help Bob, but Judy also met other spouses, who as the disease progressed, supported each other on the journey.

In the last year of his decline, he had remained at home and the only time she left the house was to buy groceries and other needed items. She felt ashamed to say she felt a bit relieved and guilty when her husband passed.

Dottie and her mother had a special bond because Dottie's father was in the military and the family had moved around often.

Dottie started talking about the fact that she and her mother were always close. They had had a silly argument about a year ago and it was emotionally painful to not talk to each other every day. When they made up after that fight, they both had agreed to always say what was bothering them rather than hold it in.

Many years were spent being in an unfamiliar state alone while he was on a mission. Being shy and having few friends, it would just be the two of them for holiday celebrations or Sunday dinners. Dottie had married in her twenties, but after twelve years of trying to make the relationship work it had ended.

Divorced and struggling to raise her teenage daughter on her own, Dottie decided to moved back home to live with her mom.

He said that at seventy-seven his life had not turned out the way he expected it to be.

Sam sat at the table looking lost. He said he had met his wife Ruth when they both attended college. Sam was going to be a lawyer and Ruth was working on becoming an accountant. At the graduation day celebration dinner with their families Sam popped the question. With tears of joy Ruth said yes and they began planning their wonderful and amazing life together.

Years of hard work and wise planning resulted in a beautiful home, two daughters and four grandchildren, who Ruth loved spoiling. Over the years Sam's practice grew and they had been able to enjoy various cruises and trips. Anyone who knew them could see they had a wonderful marriage.

Ruth started to have trouble remembering little things and had moved her accounting business to an office in their home. Driving to and from the office in town had gotten stressful when she found herself getting lost on streets she didn't intend to drive on.

While in her sixties Ruth realized she was having trouble with remembering clients' charts and when she had appointments to meet with them.

The last few years as she continued to decline, she often forgot Sam's name and had to be encouraged to get out of bed and needed assistance in eating.

When she died, Sam struggled with the loss of a fifty-six-year marriage and the love of his life, a woman he loved and cherished most of his life.

They had met on an internet dating site and in just few months had decided to get married.

Sharon said Roy was her husband from a second marriage and they had been together about fourteen years.

Sharon worked as a waitress at the local diner and Roy was a sales person at the Home Depot. He had recently been taking night classes with the hope of advancing to management. Then the Covid virus entered the US and life took a tragic turn for their household and much of the country.

Sharon's diner was forced to close as people were encouraged to stay inside their homes and quarantine with the hope of not contracting the virus themselves.

The city had all but closed up as people became fearful of the future. Sam's store, as well as many of the others, were empty most of the time and the main street looked like a ghost town.

 No longer were people spending their weekends on upgrading their homes with DIY products and Sam's commissions were shrinking as the bills were growing.

Roy grew depressed as the days turned into weeks and months of confinement. Sharon admitted Roy used to drink rather heavily, but the last few years he had been sober and attending AA meetings.

With the meetings being canceled and a poor attempt at Zoom alternatives, Sharon took the car to run a needed errand and found the beer cans in the car. Sam confessed he had been buying beer at the grocery store when he went food shopping. He promised he would stop drinking and try those Zoom meetings again. This worked for a while but one night he did not return from the store. Sharon discovered he had purchased some more beer, went to the local bridge and jumped to his death.

In the car was a note to Sharon saying he loved her very much. He had been tested at the local pharmacy and was told he had the virus. They told him it would last for a few weeks and could be mild or require hospitalization. Written in the note he said that he made a decision.

He saw no end to the craziness and didn't to want to expose his wife to the virus as she cared for him. He wanted her to find a new husband who could meet her needs and make her happy.

Sharon sobbed as she said, "I don't want another husband, I want Sam. I feel so guilty that I didn't do more to help him get through what he was feeling and feared."

Susie was a thirty-five-year-old single woman whose 18-year-old dog had to be "put to sleep".

She had become tearful when the veterinarian had told her it was best Chico no longer remain in pain. She realized it wasn't the same thing as the loss of a person, but half of her life it was just the two of them, and her whole world had revolved around him. She wanted to learn how to make her life manageable again.

Sitting in that doctor's office, her mind wandered back to how they met. Chico had been living at a dog rescue.

He was two months old and had had been abandoned by the owners of his mother because they did not want the litter of puppies.

He had been her graduation from high school present and she couldn't remember life without him. Susie had heard about a nonprofit organization called "Low Rider Dachshund Rescue of Florida". It was formed by a group of friends who were focused on the needs of the dogs, and getting information about their services and pet ownership out to the public.

Chico was just about 3 pounds when she visited the rescue and her heart just melted when she held him that first time.

A few years later when she moved out of her parents' home and into a place of her own, she made sure there was a little yard for Chico.

She has been without him for about six months now and just could not stop crying. She had not been able to get rid of his dog bed or his toys, yet whenever she held them, she became tearful. She found that she was missing work because she couldn't concentrate and sometimes skipped meals.

She said sometimes she just laid on her couch missing him. She thought attending the group may help.

Janice was the next one to speak. She said she met her husband at a high school dance and they had been married for 42 years. She was an only child and Frank was from a very large family. When he took her to his home the first time to meet his family, she felt overwhelmed.

She was not used to such a large table filled with delicious-looking food and everyone hugging her and welcoming her to their home. In a short time, she had grown to love them all and found she became good friends with his sisters. Talking with them often about her loss, she thought sometimes they grew tired of hearing her talk about him. Even with the family nearby, she admitted she often felt lonely and did not know how to live without him.

Charles was quiet and was the last one to share and he spoke softly. "My son was twenty-two when he had an accidental overdose and died.

"I knew he had been experimenting with marijuana for years but didn't know about the other drugs. This was a complete shock to my wife and I".

Charles shared that his family had been closer in the past. Tommy and his brother used to play on a semi-professional basketball team together. When Tommy's brother left for college, Tommy seemed to just withdrawal. He no longer went to play basketball saying it wasn't as fun without his brother there. Suddenly he was hanging around different people and finding excuses to stay out later than usual. When Charles tried to talk to him, he always replied that he had nothing to talk about.

As each person went around the table telling their stories the faces of the others reflected their reaction to the words. "Oh, that is so sad, what beautiful memories, I am so sorry you had to go through that alone". But the one comment they all shared was"

"I thought I was the only one!"

The only one who couldn't sleep. The only one who forgot where they were going when they left the house, or the only one who lost something simple like a set of keys.

When the counselor entered with the booklets, everyone became quiet. She introduced herself as Mary and she began to share her own story of loss.

She said everyone had their own personal story, but they all had experienced a terrible loss. The loss of someone they love and would not see in this life again.

We often use the word grief, but what is meant when someone is grieving?

Grief is the emotional response inside us when we lose someone or something that we have a bond and connection to. It affects every level of our being including physical, mental, and emotional.

Grief is a process...

Grief must be allowed to happen. Grief cannot be bypassed, hurried or rushed. It always takes longer than one expects and attempting to shorten the process invariably leads to complications and extended pain.

While the terms "grief" and "bereavement" are often used interchangeably, grief tends to be one's inside feelings whereas bereavement is the way we share with the world our expression of that loss.

Some of the ways to express bereavement can be shown in memorials, attending support groups and journal writing.

Learning to love someone and make that person a part of your life took time and patience. Learning to live without that person will also take time and patience.

Many people try to give advice to a griever following a loss. Wanting to help them feel better the advice often includes suggestions such as how long they should mourn, or how they should feel. The best advice is to follow your own heart. You will know when the time feels right for you to begin your healing journey.

Part One

Acceptance is not liking a situation. It is about acknowledging all that has been lost and learning to live with that loss."

Elizabeth Kubler-Ross and David Kessler

The Uniqueness of your Loss

Challenge One

Begin to accept the reality of the death

As each of us go through our lives, we realize things that we like and what we desire are not the same as everyone else's, this makes us unique. What does "being unique" mean?

It means that you are one of a kind and no one else is exactly like you. It comes from within. It's shown in our actions or behaviors, the way we dress, the job we have, and even the way we choose our surroundings.

Just about every restaurant you go into you will find spaghetti on the menu. On the plate you will find pasta, sauce and maybe a meatball or two.

But there are so many ways each restaurant makes theirs unique. Some people make it mild with a bit of sugar, and others like a "kick" and add something like pepperoncino or other hot chili peppers. Just like their spaghetti, their personalities are different.

That is because of their uniqueness.

Our personality begins to develop the day we are born as our temperament and behaviors start to form. Everything that happens in our lives including the good surprises and bad disappointments play a part in developing our personality.

Have you ever been in a group of people, maybe at your place of employment, and received unexpected news? Whether it was announcing you were getting the day off, or that you had to work longer hours, everyone's response will be different. This is partly because of our attitude. Attitude is defined as how we respond to people or things around us.

Hearing that you had to work late, one person might be disappointed thinking they would rather be home watching Netflix. Someone else may just think, "Oh good, a little bit of extra money in my pocket"! It all depends on the way you look at things, or your attitude.

Every one of us responds to experiences in a different way. Going on an unplanned adventure for some people would be exciting, but for others it would fill them with anxiety.

The same can be said when we experience a loss.

Some people are able to become more resilient and grow from the loss, while others struggle, retreat and wrestle with accepting a new way of life.

The people in our lives including family, friends, lovers and spouses all play a part in making us unique. They all play a role in the way we respond to things happening in our lives.

When we are going through a loss, sometimes we have people to support and comfort us, and sometimes we mourn alone. These individuals who support us in our lives have had an influence in how we learned to respond to the loss.

Dottie told the group that the close relationship between she and her mother had now transferred to Dottie and her own daughter. In the past, when fall approached, most evenings mom, Dottie and her daughter stayed home watching Christmas movies on the Hallmark channel.

When she had an opportunity to get a place of their own again, she made sure it was close to mom.

Until her death, the three of them still had their Sunday dinners as often as possible.

Janice on the other hand had a full extended family. She had married into a large family who gathered often. Holidays were always a big event and everyone could be found in the kitchen.

Whether it was preparing for a birthday or cooking the dinner of the seven fishes the room was always filled with laughter. Everyone knew if they had a problem, no matter how big or small, there was someone reaching out a hand or lending an ear to listen.

When her husband died there were people around all the time. In her childhood years she had no one to share her sadness with and kept it bottled up inside. Following Frank's death, the support continued from his family, but as her mind drifted back to her days as a teenager, she admitted she also felt hollow inside. She needed to learn how to live in the world without him.

The last trait, but maybe one of the most important is how we communicate with others. Ask yourself, are you open with your emotions and your opinion? Are you reserved and keep your feelings close inside? How is the communication between members in your own household?

How about the people you choose to be around? Are the family members and friends who are the cornerstones of your world more like Dottie's small quiet family or Judy's large expressive family?

Did something happen in your life to change the normal relationship like Tommy's brother going to college?

Being able to openly share your feelings with others following a loss can help or stifle the healing process.

If you are normally a quiet introverted person, communication with others may be difficult. If, however, you have a family that talks openly and gives you the opportunity to safely share your thoughts, healing may begin easier.

If you are quiet or do not have someone readily available to talk to there are options that help you. Journaling is one activity I started doing to help me sort my feelings. I was able to figure my thoughts out without the risk of feeling vulnerable around someone else. I do believe, however, there will come a time when you need to talk to others about your loss.

Starting in a journal or talking to someone without holding it inside is a benefit to help begin healing.

Your uniqueness is what makes you the person you are. Just how these traits play a part in your development, they also play a role in how you respond to loss.

You will have your own unique way of grieving. Everyone has the right to experience their own unique grief.

There is no right or wrong way to grieve.

Over my years as a bereavement counselor, I have found there are six challenges most survivors must travel through to find peace and comfort following their loss.

Remember, you will become a changed person after your loss. You will become part of the past and part of the future.

Why? Because, no one else will grieve in exactly the same way you do, your reactions to these challenges will be based on your own loss and you.

Denial is said to be the first stage of grief because our minds fight to believe it. Recognizing the loss by acknowledging and understanding the finality of the death is the first step.

Whether the death was sudden or anticipated, acknowledging the full reality of the loss may take weeks or months. Denial does not mean that you don't logically believe the death occurred. It is your brain protecting your body from the immense pain this will cause.

Your mind does this to help your body regulate your heart beats and blood pressure remain regular.

Tell someone about the loss today. This will help you work on this important first challenge.

One of the reasons counseling and support groups are so beneficial is that as you re-tell your story to others, and hear others share their stories, your mind is hearing and beginning to accept your loss.

You can know something in your head but not in your heart. This is what often happens when someone you love dies. So, the first challenge of mourning involves gently confronting the reality that someone you care about will never physically come back into your life again.

Allowing yourself to embrace this painful reality of the death is not quick, easy or well-organized. As you begin to grow from your current loss, it may be helpful to look at your life up to this point, and remember how you responded to previous losses.

Were you and your family raised to embrace and celebrate those who have died, or to never discuss them following a funeral? What were your ritual or funeral experiences?

For some, funerals are not seen as a closure, but more as a beginning. A beginning of their lives in eternity and for us to begin living on earth without them.

Funerals are an event that help with the acceptance challenge. This can be a solemn time or one with many people, music and food. The uniqueness of the funeral can be seen in the rituals of the survivors.

My aunt had married an undertaker who owned a funeral home. When my grandparents died the service was held there and open to the town. They had lived most of their lives in this town, and many friends wished to pay their respects.

Following the service, the family retreated to the parlor as food and conversations were shared of the fond memories they experienced growing up with my grandparents.

When my best friend's father died the service was quiet and solemn. A service was held at their church with no gathering to follow.

Both are acceptable and are a result of your uniqueness and the family choices.

Looking back over the years, I had found the funerals of my loved ones were comforting, but were simply about the day they left the earth.

My family members did not acknowledge current birthdays, anniversaries of the death, or include them in conversations after that day.

Even with my family traditions ingrained in me, over time I developed my own beliefs and those loved ones have continued to be in my heart, thoughts, traditions and memories.

Asking the members of the group to share their funeral experience may seem cruel, but it is in fact a much-needed step in completing our first challenge, which is learning to accept our loss.

Cathy's eyes filled with tears as she shared the days leading up to her mother's funeral and that day. Mom became sick during the pandemic and family members and friends were not allowed to visit the assisted living community. They were only allowed to visit through the windows. This was a terrible way to visit because of her mother's loss of hearing and increasing dementia.

She smiled as a memory came to mind when she "fibbed" to the staff that her mother had an appointment with a local doctor and she took her to her own house for a birthday dinner for mom with all of her children. She knew it might be wrong, but mom was declining and wanted to see her children on more time. They needed to see her as well.

No one was allowed to attend the funeral service at her favorite church. The service was offered on Zoom through the church website and family and friends were given a link and time to watch. Because of the Zoom funeral, the reality of the death was easily dismissed by Cathy who was used to her mom living away from her. The closure and acceptance were still a lingering concern.

Sam let a tear slide down his face as he started to talk about Ruth's funeral. She had been an accountant for several years and it seemed like everyone she ever helped was there to pay their respects. Family and friends spoke of what she had meant to them and how she had made their lives better.

Judy and her husband had made his pre-arrangements due to his illness. They had planned a simple service in the chapel of their local funeral home. She admitted that for some that may sound morbid, but it was in fact quite a comfort.

The service was beautiful and just what her husband wanted. He had helped pick out a Bible passage that meant something to him, his favorite hymns and the closing prayer. Doing this left Judy feeling blessed for her life with him and comforted that he had helped with everything and it was what he wanted. She admitted that making all of these arrangements herself following his death would have been emotionally draining on her.

Dottie's dad had been in the military and he was awarded benefits to be buried in the memorial military cemetery. Spouses are offered the same benefits and are often able to be buried next the veteran. A local funeral home provided the arrangements. Dottie was thankful for her father's service and the military's financial support. The staff of the funeral home said this was one way of thanking the men and women who were in the military for their service.

Sharon said her first husband's funeral was like Dottie's dad's in that it was performed by a military funeral home.

Held in the chapel on the base where they had been stationed. Because it was never recovered, there was no body at the service.

Friends living on the base attended and the chaplain read the eulogy and she was left alone to grieve.

Roy's funeral was a closed casket and no one attended except Sharon. His parents were deceased and his co-workers had not been in contact. She was grieving again without support from others during the pandemic.

This time she fought to understand why someone commits suicide instead of asking for help. She hoped to learn about that during the group meetings.

Rumors and gossip filled the neighborhood about his actions and her relationship with Roy. Following his funeral her own feelings and actions were questioned by many of the town people and she silently cried alone.

Slipping into her own depression she had not returned to work, but was now here at the group asking for help from others.

Suzie was quiet during this discussion. She said she was feeling like she shouldn't talk about her dog's death.

Cathy told her that although the others had come to the group for the loss of a person, she too had lost a pet and knew the emotional bond created with our pets.

Suzie shared that she had Chico cremated and the urn was in her home. Her parents came over the day she received the urn and they shared stories of his life and memories they would always remember.

Janice let out a small laugh as she said our funeral was not as somber as many of yours. The family gathered in the church and yes, there were songs and bible readings, but it was a celebration of her husband going to be with the Lord.

Family and friends had spent hours eating, drinking, telling stories and sharing about the wonderful person that was Frank. She did admit that following that emotional day, she missed him even more and continued to grieve his absence.

Charles admitted humbly he did not have a service for his son. When Tommy died, he was embarrassed that his son had been using drugs.

The family had decided to have a closed service and they rarely spoke about the death or even Tommy.

After attending our group sessions, he now understood that he was punishing himself, Tommy's family and friends by not letting them openly mourn. He also realized that they had punished themselves for one day of his life rather than remembering the other twenty-two years of their life with him.

Each one of the group members were taking notes and remembering their uniqueness and that of the people in their lives.

It is not only your personality, but the personality of the person who died and what else is going on in your lives at the time of the death that can affect your grief.

Learn to embrace the uniqueness of your grief. Your grief is yours alone. The past losses and how you feel about them is yours alone. Things like how long it took to begin healing in the past, your relationship with the person and the circumstances surrounding their death all play an important role in how you handled past losses in your life. These experiences and events will also play a role in how you heal this time, and how you will move forward.

Losses in your life

Losses in our lives are not limited to the people we love. Losing a pet, a home a job, or even moving to a new area can all be seen as emotional losses. Completing your own personal loss history may include divorces, job losses, mental and physical illnesses, and major moves.

When anything that is precious or important to us is taken away, we experience a loss and we grieve for what was and for what might have been. With each loss think back to your reaction, emotions and feelings at the time and how you felt at the time.

You have the right to talk about your grief. Talking about your grief will help you heal. Seek out others who will allow you to talk as much as you want, share as much as you want, and as often as you want about your grief.

Secondary losses

When we lose someone we love, we not only lose their physical self, but we may also lose other secondary tasks as well. Some of those losses are internal and affect us personally. Others are external ones and affect the world around us.

Self or a loss of identity – Maybe you were a daughter or son, maybe a spouse, or a parent. Whatever word described your relationship is now gone.

The identity you shared is now a part of your past. Some people loved being linked to that role and find themselves grieving that loss.

Self-confidence – Without the reinforcement from our loved one, some people experience the failure to recognize their own personal wholeness. This feeling can lead to feelings of inadequacy and not believing they can do anything right.

The Ability to focus and make decisions – When the brain is so consumed with thinking about our pain and the loss, focusing on what seems to be the "non-essentials" seems unimportant. This is because our entire being is now affected by the loss. This insecurity and lack of trust in ourselves can cause us to look to others for direction and advice.

The Ability to see choices – When we experience such a monumental loss we may feel out of control. We may feel in a sense that we have no control over anything in our life.

A Sense of humor, happiness or joy- Feeling guilty for laughing or having fun we may fail to see anything as funny or believe feeling happy is wrong because one of the most important people in one's life is no longer around. There may be difficulty in recognizing happiness in one's own life

Health – Our own self-care often declines following the loss of someone we love, and may affect our own health. The emotional stress and strain of grief work can cause physical problems such as nausea, migraine headaches, muscle knots and back problems.

Patience with self – Sometimes a grieving person does not believe they should feel good. They may fight the desire to feel better leaving them with feelings of inadequacy and failure.

A Chosen lifestyle – You may have spent years building your life the way you wanted it to be. The living arrangements, friends and even your working situation may change after a loss. You are now being forced to begin a new way of life when it wasn't your decision or choice.

Security – When you have lost a spouse who worked or contributed to the financial security of the household, the uncertainty of not knowing what to expect in the future can be difficult. You may not know what will happen next, or how to emotionally react or respond to this loss.

The Past – Following a loss you may find support from old friends and some new friends. Although they can be supportive of your loss, the new friends do not know the history of the two of you. The lack of knowledge to the grieving person's past journey can make comforting you harder.

The Future and future dreams – The future was once something joyful to anticipate, but has now become fearful. It now may be hard to be thinking ahead or even imagining next year or next month or next week without your loved one.

The dreams of spending the rest of your life with them, seeing your parent become a grandmother or see that child grow up is now gone. Instead, there is the underlying fear that the future will be just as painful as the present moment.

Sharing with a loved one – One of the daily secondary losses is not having someone to listen to the little things and big events of your day-to-day living. The loss of all the firsts of your child in their growing up years.

Without intentional intervention actions, these feelings of grief can last for two to five years. However, finding alternative thoughts and creating new plans of recourse, can help reduce the negative thoughts and find positive opportunities.

The secondary losses listed may surprise the survivors. Often the first few days and even weeks can be filled with funeral arrangements and emotional feelings and they may not even come to mind. Over the next few months some of these losses may soon become apparent.

After giving the group the next handout assignment, Mary asked them to take the list and pick out two of them that they could relate to. She encouraged them to share the answers with the group the next time they met.

Writing Exercise:

What are some of the secondary losses have you experienced?

_____

_____

_____

_____

_____

_____

_____

_____

Dottie selected the loss of the past. She admitted she never asked her mother about her life as a child and growing up before she was born. She just kept wishing she had taken up the gentleman's offer to do a video with her mom.

They were called lifetime legacies and included pictures and interviews with the person about their life. She remembered she used to have fun times with her mother that included laughing and having dinners with her mom, daughter and herself.

Cathy felt she had experienced a loss of a large chunk of self, the loss of her identity and had lost her self-confidence. Being her mother's caregiver had been her identity for so long.

She admitted she didn't know how to just be "Cathy".

Meal choices had been determined by what mom could eat. Television shows were always a show from years gone by that mom remembered. Kathy admitted she didn't even know what kind of music she liked since it always been the music of days gone by that they would listen to in the car and house.

Because their relationship was so intertwined, Cathy often asked her mother to help her with decisions and had come to rely on that.

Suzie selected the loss of a sense of humor, happiness or joy. Her life had been filled with memories of Chico for all of her adult life.

Waking up to "puppy kisses" even when Chico was getting gray hair started her day off brighter. Just walking in the door from work to see him running towards her had made the day better. Co-workers told her she should get another dog, but she could not even imagine finding happiness with another four-legged friend.

Sharon found after her husband's death she had lost some of her ability to focus, to see choice options and to make financial decisions with just her income.

She admitted she feels lost without her husband. They used to make all their decisions together and now she found she questioned her decisions and didn't know how to make them alone.

Most of her time was focused on thinking about the empty side of the bed. What to do with his clothes, how to exist in the world as a single person when she used to be part of a couple.

Janice and her husband had lived a very lavish life. Living in one of the nicer areas of town they frequented the country club for dinner often.

Frank had been in one job most of his life and had a sizable pension and retirement income. Janice would lose much of that income now that her husband had passed. Her lifestyle would drastically change.

Charles was the first one to bring up the loss of health and also felt a loss of future dreams. Charles admitted he was not eating or sleeping properly and had spent far too many hours at work trying not to think about what happened to his son. He had also begun to have headaches and heartbreaking dreams.

Charles said he picked the loss of the future as the one that hurt him the most. He always hoped his son would find a woman and they would have children that he would have the pleasure of watching grow and enjoy. He also admitted he lost the future of his son getting off drugs. He wished that he would have seen this was not a way to live and seek help.

The financial responsibilities and accumulated debt of caring for her husband and his illness had climbed to an unthinkable amount.

Judy said the loss she felt connected to most was the loss of a chosen lifestyle and the lack of patience with herself.

Living alone she had thought about moving to a smaller place, maybe a condo that didn't require as much maintenance. Unfortunately, the extra mortgage that was taken out of the house would leave very little profits and she would have to move to a much smaller place then she desired. Not only would she be giving up her home, she would be moving away from her church that she had been going to for years and leaving friends.

Judy said her husband not only gave her love and purpose, but he gave her validation she was doing a good job at providing his care. He was her biggest cheerleader and with him now gone, she thinks maybe she lacks the patience and confidence to believe in herself.

Sam said his losses began years ago as Ruth's dementia began to decline further. The secondary loss he connected with the most was the loss of his own health.

When she did not want to eat, he felt funny eating in front of her. His sleep habits had also been interrupted because of fears of her getting out of bed and wandering. Now living alone, he finds he has not been able to return to his healthy self-care habits.

All eight of them admitted they missed things like

coming home from work and sharing the news of their day. Going on an outing, going to visit or even calling on the phone their loved one. This was no longer something to look forward to and the void was a large one.

Becoming Me After You

Part Two

Grief is like the ocean; it comes on waves ebbing and flowing. Sometimes the water is calm, and sometimes it is overwhelming. All we can do is learn to swim."

Vicki Harrison

Exploring your Feelings and Emotions

Challenge Two

Give yourself permission to begin letting yourself feel the pain of the loss

Once you have begun to accept the loss, comes the time to allow yourself to feel your emotions. Reacting to the changes involves experiencing the pain, feeling, identifying, accepting, and expressing your reactions to the loss.

Although you may emotionally fight it and try to avoid it, you must begin to embrace the pain of the loss.

Reach out and spend time with someone who doesn't try to take your pain and sense of loss away. Remember this is not out of selfishness, they may feel helpless and are unable to ease your sadness.

Although Janice, Sharon and Judy had all lost their husbands, their situations and recovering from the loss took different paths.

Judy had provided total care for her husband since he began to decline a few years ago. When he first was diagnosed there were friends and neighbors who offered support and an empathetic ear. Once he declined more rapidly, they stopped visiting and calling.

Some of her friends even urged her to stop crying because there was nothing she could do. When he was rushed to the hospital with complication she visited alone. Two days later when he died, hospital staff told her that at least he was no longer suffering.

Judy admitted she found sometimes she was agreeing that his passing was a relief. She discovered she was having moments of being glad it was all over. Other times, she realized the life she had known and loved for so long, was now over, and depression and tears began to surface.

Janice felt lost without her husband. From the minute they woke up and began their day they had been together.

She couldn't believe he had been on a ladder outside in their yard when he fell after passing out.

She kept saying to friends, "If I only had hired someone to do that job, he would still be with me." With little warning he was admitted to the hospital and subsequently died there. She had no time to prepare for a life without him.

Sharon was younger and had not been with Roy for a long time compared to the others in the group. She had been alone before and thought she could handle the pain. Thinking this death would not affect her the same way her first husbands had, she was surprised at the waves of emotions she felt. Her first husband had been killed in the line of duty and his body was never recovered. For years her mind played tricks on her that maybe he wasn't dead and would return to her.

Although there was a body this time, her mind continued to play tricks on her. Sometimes she would awake thinking he was at work.

To begin healing we need to first mourn our loss. To do that requires us first to accept the death and then to embrace the pain of our loss –to confront it.

This can be exhausting and mentally draining. During this time, you may need to sometimes take a break and distract yourself from the pain of death. Other times you will need to create a safe place to move toward it.

As you encounter your pain, you will also need to nurture yourself physically, emotionally and spiritually. Eat well, rest often and exercise regularly. Find others with whom you can share your painful thoughts and feelings. Talk with friends who listen without judging, they are your most important helpers as you work on this mourning need.

Some people find comfort in their faith and others struggle after a death. Give yourself permission to question your faith. It's OK to be angry with your God and to struggle with "meaning of life" issues at this time.

Humans are said to be the only species that cry emotional tears.

As anyone who has cooked with onions knows, peeling them produces tears.

Scientists have discovered that there is a different chemical compound in tears shed by someone who has lost a loved one, or someone who is in physical pain. Why do we feel better after we have had a "good cry"?

It is because emotion-filled tears are said to remove toxic chemicals from the body following a sensitive crisis. In doing so, tears restore our emotional balance.

The hormones released as one cries in sadness release endorphins and give you a calmer feeling afterwards. Onion's tears do not have the same effect.

Crying is something that some people are conditioned to do, where others are discouraged to weep. This can be based on family traditions and expectations and our own personality. Adults cry less than children, and men tend to cry less than women. Is this a product of conditioning or biology? I am not sure.

If you are prone to cry, remember, there is no need to deprive yourself of this natural healthy release of your emotions, but know that not everyone feels a need to cry.

Not crying does not signify that you are not grieving or do not care. In the same context, uncontrolled crying does not mean you are going crazy.

Feelings of helplessness and hopelessness are common following a loss and for some, tears may begin to fall.

Judy raised her hand to speak, with a slight smile she said she was a retired substitute teacher and always taught her students not to blurt out or interrupt others. She said she was so glad to hear this because she had been comparing herself to her friend Robin and thought there was something wrong with herself.

Robin sobbed all the time. Whenever they would get together for coffee, she would be fine but suddenly something would be brought up in the conversation and she would suddenly begin crying.

She admitted she had been tearful at times, but over the last few months had found she slept better since he passed away. She didn't need to worry any longer about her husband falling or wandering away in the middle of the night. She admitted Robin was making her feel bad for not crying.

Sam shared with the group that he may have been cried out since getting the diagnosis. He didn't like to show his tears in public but for months as she was sleeping and declining, he quietly cried.

For people like Judy and Sam, who may have begun grieving and shedding tears when they received the news of the prognosis the acceptance can come sooner.

Mary explained what Suzie was experiencing may be something called "Grief Bubbles or Bursts". This happens when you are overcome by emotion, thinking about the loss you have experienced. It can be triggered by a memory, a song, a smell, or other things.

She shared that she often experiences them when she hears a song on the radio that her dad used to sing to her when she was young.

Crying can also begin when you see a person who resembles your loved one or has their mannerisms. These can all trigger the floodgates to open. Crying can be a few tears or a seemingly forever non-stop episode. Be gentle with yourself and if tears begin to fall, allow the tears to flow if they need to.

Suzie said she felt like she was on a rollercoaster with her emotions and feelings. So many of her co-workers told her Chico was just a pet and she should stop feeling sorry for herself. Many of them were not dog or cat owners and did not understand her deep affection for him.

It is important to let your feelings out.

You have the right to feel any and all of a multitude of emotions. Confusion, disorientation, fear, guilt and relief are just a few of the emotions you might feel during your grief journey.

Others may try to tell you what you are feeling is wrong. Maybe telling you that you have no reason to be angry. Don't take these judgmental responses to heart. Instead, find empathetic listeners who will accept your feelings without condition.

Someone experiencing a loss may have emotions that come and go, only to repeat themselves again. Four of the common feelings many experiences after a loss include anger, guilt, depression and regret.

You may be angry, even outraged that this has happened and "ruined" your life. You may become fearful that you won't be able to cope, and may fall apart.

Janet admitted she got filled with anger that Frank died. He had done everything for her, saying it was his privilege and honor to do it. She was now faced with no idea how to handle the finances and no one to hold hands with during a movie.

She admitted trying to find someone to fix a leaky faucet and mow the grass, but she found herself frustrated and said that frustration sometimes turned to a tearful anger. Feeling sad, frustrated or even angry at times is understandable.

Something important to you has ended – a relationship with someone you love. You may doubt that life will be as good as it once was. Our feelings arise from very deep within us and are ours alone and these feelings matter to us.

If we have been conditioned or simply feel we should hold our emotions in, thinking it will go away, it won't happen. It will not help to bottle up your feelings, keeping them tightly sealed inside. One of the reasons for this is if left unmanaged, the pressure may actually build up and demand to be released in an inappropriate place or situation.

Charles has been raised to be stoic and not show how difficult the loss of his son had been on him. He spent more hours at work and always seemed to be doing something to keep busy.

He shared with the group that while grocery shopping one day he overheard a father and son arguing about what to buy for dinner.

Remembering a night watching a basketball game on TV and eating pizza together, a grief burst erupted and he shouted "Quit your yelling, at least you have a son to eat dinner with".

He suddenly realized that he had not accepted his loss or talked to anyone about how it affected him. Apologizing to the other man and his son, he said to them, "Maybe I should talk to a close friend of find a support group".

Feelings of guilt may be experienced by a survivor for many reasons. Family caregivers who have spent months and possibly even years watching someone they love slowly decline may experience relief guilt.

Feeling relieved they no longer have to provide care or put their life on hold often results in mixed emotions and guilt.

Even though Judy's friends understood that Bob was not well, they really didn't understand how hard it was for her to deal with. She admitted she felt guilt when she had to stay home with him, guilty when she left, and guilty for feeling relieved the struggle was over.

Do you have any feelings of guilt? Was there anything you could have done to change the outcome?

A definition for caregiver burnout is defined as "being in a state of physical, emotional and mental exhaustion. It may be accompanied by a change in attitude, from positive and caring to negative and unconcerned. Burnout can occur when caregivers don't get the help they need, or if they try to do more than they are able, physically or financially".

This is what happened to Cathy and why the loss of her mother is so difficult.

Cathy told the group that working full time and raising teenage children was hard enough for her to balance, but now she had a new responsibility, her mother.

It began with calls to her at work asking if she would stop on the way home and bring her something from the store. The occasional stops turned into daily visits to make sure mom was taking her medications and caring for herself.

She admitted to feeling annoyed that she could no longer meet her girlfriends for dinner or enjoy a quiet night after work. Looking back now, she would give anything for one more phone call from her mother asking her to stop by. Leaving work now she finds herself feeling depressed that the part of her life that took so much time was now over.

Depression is one of the most common and longest lasting feelings following the loss of someone you love. Wishing to be left alone and giving in to your grief is understandable. Not knowing what the future holds for you can be hard.

Sensing that your world has been changed forever can leave someone feeling vulnerable.

Giving into your sadness for a while is acceptable but finding ways to leave those emotions behind will help you to begin to heal from your loss.

Everyone at the table admitted to having depression at times. Mary said this is understandable for anyone experiencing a loss. She reminded them that they had loved the person for a long time and had them in their heart. To continue life without them on earth but to keep them in their heart is the goal.

She encouraged them to embrace and allow those depression times to surface for they are part of the journey towards acceptance. The goal, is to not remain in the depression for extended periods of time. She would show them activities to help relieve and reduce those times.

Regrets are often experienced when you didn't have a chance to tell them good-bye or say something you always wanted to say to them.

Maybe it was something you held back saying, something that now leaves you with an empty feeling inside.

Cathy said she probably had the most regrets in the group. The arguments with her mother were over something simple. So simple she couldn't remember it after that day.

After giving everyone a chance to talk Mary handed them each two pieces of paper.

Writing Exercise:

On the first one she instructed them to write about something they wished they had said but held inside. Write about an argument that never was resolved, or a request that was never fulfilled?

_____

_____

_____

_____

_____

_____

_____

Every one of them had started with saying they wished they had told them "I love you" one more time. But the answers also slowly became more personal.

Dottie said she wished she had told her mother how much she appreciated everything she had done for her when she took her and her daughter in after the divorce.

Being a mom herself now, she now understood unconditional love and the sacrifices we make for our children.

Sharon wished she had told Roy they could work together to find a solution to the current difficult situation. Many people were able to get assistance for housing and food needs during covid. His insurance from Home Depot would have covered the medical costs and the hospitals were filled with essential workers trained to help those infected.

Sam spoke up next and said he and Ruth had never argued, something that surprised many of their friends. He did however wish he had more memories with Ruth before her dementia took over her mind.

Judy grew misty when she said, "I would have told him it was ok to go to the lord. He fought so hard with his illness because he didn't want me to be alone. He thought he had to be strong for me."

Cathy was quite for a minute and gently spoke. "I would have told my mom as much as I wanted to, I couldn't keep her at my home. I would have said I was sorry I couldn't have met her care needs myself and had to place her to the care community.

Sometimes I think back and worry she thought I sent her away because she was too much trouble."

Charles hadn't spoken often in the group but said he wished he had been closer and in better contact with his son. Once Tommy had reached adulthood, he thought constant contact came across as meddling and intrusive rather than caring and concerned.

Janice was the last one to speak and shared saying she wished she had told her husband not to go outside. That they had hired a lawn person. She wished she had told him how much he had made their life wonderful and what a loving husband he was.

Mary thanked them for their loving answers and said that unresolved grief or things we wish we had said or didn't say can often keep grievers from healing.

Writing Exercise:

She then asked them to write a letter to the person to acknowledge their painful feelings.

Dear...

• I remember when you...

• The hardest part about your death is...

• It would have been nice if...

• I'm really sorry for...

• My best time with you was...

_____

_____

_____

_____

_____

Part Three

"Deep grief sometimes is almost like a specific location, or a coordinate on a map of time. When you are standing in that forest of sorrow, you cannot imagine that you could ever find yourself to in a better place. But if some person, someone can assure you that they themselves have stood in that very same spot, and now have moved on, sometimes this event will bring you hope."

Elizabeth Gilbert

Memories and Misconceptions

Challenge Three

Actively begin remembering the person who died.

Over time, neuroscience has discovered that those who have experienced the loss of a loved one can learn to experience something called emotional healing.

An article I read in Psychology Today confirmed what anyone experiencing loss can attest to, that emotional pain is just as real as physical pain.

Just like our body can regenerate from a physical pain, the heart and mind can also heal from the emotional pain.

Although not in the same way as we would heal from a broken leg, this is done when the brain replaces the painful images associated with the loss with new images.

The new ones encourage and motivate a new behavior that promote growth and well-being of the survivor. For most people this happens naturally, but for others it can take quite a while.

Newly experienced emotional pain can be intense and overwhelming. The feelings of loss are amplified and can consume most of someone's thoughts.

Over time the mind shifts from that severe pain to allow positive memories to enter.

The sad and painful visions are replaced with positive memories of time spent with the deceased loved one. Although many grieving people would disagree, there will be a time when it becomes enjoyable to think about the lost loved one.

A positive image is brought to your mind using your imagination that eases pain by shifting your mental focus from loss to growth. This image can be something you've seen, heard, smelled, or touched.

Cathy listened intensely to what was being said and chimed in that the sudden and completely unexpected death of her mother turned her world upside down.

In the weeks and months after her death it hurt so much to think of her that she avoided all sentimental reminders of her – photos were packed away, her favorite things were stored in the closet, and the music she loved was changed to a different channel on the stereo.

She was not successful in suppressing the grieving feelings with a house full of empty pictures and belongings, and brought them all back out. She still missed her mother and believed her dying was the darkest day of her life.

Practicing the exercise discussed, Cathy returned a month later to say it had worked a little bit for her. She had come to realize that the most important thing in her life was not her mother's death, but was the time they spent together and memories she had in her heart and mind.

When she was feeling sad, she mentally applied the positive, happy times she spent together with her mom.

Charles said it was very hard to accept his son's death because not only had he lost the future days they would share; he lost the opportunity to make things between them better once more.

When we lose loved ones, we don't lose everything we ever experienced with them. All that we lose is the future with them.

He closed his eyes and let his mind drift to memories in the past. Remembering days of his family gathering and watching his sons play basketball.

Emotional healing begins when we begin to focus more on the many positive memories and experiences, we had with them. These are something we will never lose.

Mary instructed the group that between today's session and the next meeting, when in a safe place and calm state, to make a list of their more prominent painful memories.

She suggested they practice associating at least one of their restorative images with each item on the list every day, until the new associations become automatic.

She said if it doesn't work the first time don't get discouraged. It should be easier over time.

In learning this changed way of thinking, you are remembering the person who's gone but they stay on through our memories.

It is fine to include both the unhappy and happy times, but also to focus on what you can change at this time. Continue to display those pictures if they bring you comfort as they help you stay out of denial and let you remember those you love.

We are living in a culture that teaches us that to move away from – instead of toward – our grief is the best answer. I disagree.

I think it is good for you to remember the past because it makes hoping for the future possible.

Do you think you have any kind of relationship with someone after they die?

Of course, you do! You have a relationship of memory.

Precious memories, dreams reflecting the significance of the relationship, and objects that link you to the person who has died are all examples of some of the things that give testimony to a different form of a continued relationship.

Writing Exercise:

Write as fast as you can for ten minutes listing traits or memories of the person who is gone. Put away the list for future reflection when you wish to practice restorative thinking.

_____

_____

_____

_____

_____

_____

_____

_____

Here are few examples of things you can do to keep memories alive while embracing the reality that the person has died:

• Talking with someone or writing out your favorite memories

• yourself "permission" to keep some special keepsakes or "linking objects"

•Displaying photos of the person who died.

•Visiting places of special significance that stimulate memories of times shared together

•Looking at photo albums at special times such as holidays, birthdays and anniversaries.

Memories are your mind's way of visually holding close people, places and events that are in your heart. The special relationship you shared with the one you love who has now passed began the day you met and did not end the day he or she died.

For months and years to come, those memories of times together will bring you both comfort and tears.

Writing Exercise:

Mary asked them to bring a photo of their choosing. She also asked them to write about any personal items of their loved one they have now as keepsakes? How do these items make you feel?

_____

_____

_____

_____

_____

_____

_____

When they returned the next month, it was obvious the eight strangers had started to become friends. The conversations were more relaxed and each person was greeted with smiles as they shared their photo and story.

Charles passed a picture around of himself, his two boys and wife at a major league basketball game All were smiling and he said this was a great day and memory. Holding the picture, he pointed to the shirt he was wearing and shared a slight grin. Although we were thirty years apart in age, we wore the same size. I have many of his t-shirts that tell his life over the years. I hold them, smell them, sometimes sleep with one and remember him. I know he is not on earth anymore but as I hug the shirts, I think he knows I am sending him a hug to heaven.

Cathy brought a picture of her parents on their wedding day. It was obvious she took after her mother because the picture could have been Cathy herself.

She said before she passed, her mother gave her the wedding rings she and her father got married with. It was a gold band with two very small diamonds due to the struggles of the times. Shaped in hearts, Cathy said it signified the joining of their two hearts. As she showed them to everyone she said "They may not be worth much at the jewelers, but to me they are priceless".

Dottie had a picture of her own baptism with her mother holding her. She said she had that baptism outfit because her mother had given it to Dottie when she gave birth to her own daughter. Faded and tattered over time, she could still remember that day she gave it to her and other times that were special to her even now.

Janice showed everyone a group of people gathered for Franks retirement dinner. She still had her husband's watch. Every morning he would put it on and smile. The watch had been a gift from his employer on the day he retired. It signified the years of providing for Janice and their family. As the watch ticked, she said wearing it she felt close to him.

Sharon reminded the group that she had met Roy on the internet.

They had spent hours on-line talking about favorite movies and music.

The picture she shared was of them when they went to a musical concert. Roy had made her a flash-drive with all the songs from the concert that they listened to. She plays it at home and even sometimes in the car. When she hears the special ones, she can vision him in front of her singing them and she now smiles through her tears.

Sam had brought a filled photo album of their wedding day to the group meeting. He said he sits and looks at the pictures often and they bring him comfort. Remembering how beautiful she was and that special glow she had. He grew a bit giddy as he told us she said her blushing was from her excitement in becoming his wife.

Suzie brought two pictures with her that day. One was Chico the first day she brought him home, and the second was last Christmas with them both in front of the Christmas tree. She said she also had the urn so she felt Chico was with her always. She also had the first collar she bought him when he was just a few pounds.

She sometimes wears it on her wrist like a bracelet when she had trouble sleeping.

Judy had her favorite picture of them on vacation. She said the last few years had been primarily providing care for her husband, but before that they went on amazing trips and cruises. She would now sit in the early evening hours and look at the pictures he painted of their adventures. Seeing them bending upside down to kiss the Blarney Stone or dancing together on formal night on the last night of their Alaskan cruise made her smile.

Misconceptions

A misconception is a conclusion that's wrong because it's based on faulty thinking or facts. Often at the time we believe they are correct because we don't know differently. Maybe it's a belief that was handed down for generations or maybe it is a way someone is conditioned to believe.

Here are a few misconceptions about that grief that may hinder the healing process.

Misconception: It has been six months - you should be over this by now.

Truth: You will never "be over" this pain. The pain never completely leaves. Only you can determine how long you will mourn. You will spend your entire lifetime missing your departed love ones. You may however, learn some skills to assist you in dealing with your pain.

Grief is physically exhausting and mentally draining. One of the keys to healing is accepting and embracing the intensity of your grief. Understand it being a normal reaction to one of the most difficult experiences a human could experience.

This acceptance and healing may be derailed by friends, family, and their own misconceptions and false beliefs. Even if they are having the best of intentions, they could cause you to continue to suffer longer.

Misconception: The length of time you were with them makes a difference in your grief.

If you were with them a short time the less intense your pain should be.

Truth: The reality is that the love for a parent, spouse or child is not contingent upon the amount of time you had with them. Love simply cannot be measured in time. Would it have been easier to experience the loss one year later? No. There is never an easier time with a lesser pain. It is a horrible experience whenever it happens.

Misconception: Sleeping pills, antidepressants or alcohol will help to get you through this pain.

Truth: Some doctors are quick to advise someone to take pills to try to hide the pain. People may also use alcohol after the death in an attempt to dull their pain. Eventually these people will realize that they may have just been postponing the inevitable.

Misconception: You need to "Be strong"

Truth: Appearing strong and denying your feelings will only keep you from accepting and healing your heart.

Misconception: Support groups are for weak people.

Truth: The death of someone can be one of the most isolating and lonely events experienced. You may begin wondering if your friends could possibly help. You may also wonder if anyone else could understand the depth of this pain if they have never experienced it before?

This is why support groups help. Support groups are a safe haven for people to share the deepest of their pain with others who have experienced the same feelings.

Misconception: It is best to avoid discussing the loss

Truth: The grieving survivor needs and wants to talk about their loss, including the smallest details connected to it.

Compassionate Friends used to say "Grief shared is grief diminished". Each time a griever talks about the loss, a layer of pain is shed.

Misconception: Hold your emotions inside long enough and they will go away. Telling you that once you start sharing your feelings, the feelings may come out in anger, depression, physical illness, and even addictive behaviors.

Truth: Friends may encourage you to hold your grief inside. People do not like to see you grieving and we are often taught to move away from our grief, not towards it. It is important to grieve openly with others who are compassionate and empathetic as well as alone when needing to.

Misconception: Grief travels in 5 stages.

Truth: There is no straight line through the stages to grief. You may feel denial or anger at one point and once that moment leaves you think it's over.

Unfortunately, you may find it resurfaces weeks later. You will most likely weave in and out of the stages as you search for comfort.

Misconception: Keep busy on holidays, anniversaries, and birthdays.

Truth: Many people continue to honor their loved one on those days. It is not a "backsliding" as some would believe. It is letting that memory and your love remain.

Misconception: Most people "recover" from grief and return to a normal life.

Truth: After you lose someone your life will never return to normal. You will learn to develop a new "normal" that will incorporate your past life and all those memories, memories that you will treasure along with the new memories you will be building.

Misconception: After you survived that first year it will be better.

Truth: There is no magic date that life will become better. Sometimes the second year can be more difficult because the denial is gone. Although acceptance may have begun, there are new situations and experiences that at times may cause those previous emotions and feelings to return.

Holidays and birthdays without the ones we love can be difficult. Seeing other families enjoying themselves may cause a grieving person to retreat to their home alone. Not wishing unhappiness for others, but being filled with sadness, pain, anger or dread they grieve alone.

Grief can magnify the normal stress a holiday carries, as one is filled with memories of past holidays and with uncertainty for the future ones.

At holiday time it is important to give yourself permission to feel whatever you are experiencing. So often grieving people do what others want or expect of them and are then filled with resentment or anger. If you feel sad and want to cry, then do it. If you are angry, find a safe way to vent your feelings.

Don't be afraid to ask for help during these special days and holidays. You know the friends you can call who will never consider you a burden.

In reality, it often makes others feel better when they are asked for help. Ask someone to help with cooking, shopping, or decorating when you are experiencing an emotional day.

Does it feel right to have a birthday party or cake when they are not here?? Does having a gathering and talking about them bring comfort? Don't do anything you don't feel like doing and give yourself time to heal. You don't have to pretend to be having fun, but if a glimmer of smiles or happiness finds its way into your life – enjoy the moment.

Part Four

"Although it's natural to forget your power after you lose a loved one, the truth is that after a break-up, divorce, or a death, there remains an ability within you to create a new reality."

Louise Hay and David Kessler

Getting Past the Past

Challenge Four
Begin finding ways to learn from our loss

From the moment you lost your loved one, everything changed. Your current lifestyle and the hopes and any plans for the future now seem uncertain.

For many people including myself, the hardest part of getting past the past was accepting and learning from the loss. We know in our brains that what has happened has already taken place... but we often play tricks with our heart.

Accept and learn from the past

One suggestion is to think about your relationship and your time together and begin to look at some of the benefits of having this person in your life. As you are beginning to accept the loss of this person what are the emotions you are feeling?

Ask yourself how these feelings can be used to empower yourself now and in the future. Once you have finished thinking and writing down your thoughts, give your mind a rest. This exercise will not be a one-time assignment.

Just because you have begun to accept things have happened does not mean you have to like it.

Do this in small doses. Reflecting on the past for a little bit of time is acceptable, however, continued dwelling on it will only keep those negative thoughts and feelings around.

Feel Your feelings

Many people try to keep their feelings inside because it is too emotional to let them out. It is important to get those feelings out of your brain, but it is also good for your health. Holding onto your feelings leads to anxiety, depression, headache and high blood pressure. A good place to start is to describe the degree of your emotions, and share them with someone who will listen and not pass judgement.

Let it go and learn to forgive

Stop blaming others for your pain and forgive them. Begin to forgive yourself as well.

No one is perfect and we all make mistakes. Instead of kicking yourself for your past mistakes, cut yourself some slack and focus on the lessons that you've learned. Once you're not carrying that anger and resentment around, you'll be able to move on.

Playing the role of the victim is easy, especially when compared to accepting the truth. The problem is, blaming others and yourself prevents you from going forward.

Surround yourself with support

Although you may have a lot of people around you offering to help, take an inventory of them. Are there people who are negative or not interested in hearing your story? You may be surprised at the ones who are there to help you. This may be a good opportunity to meet new people by going to a local meet-up, support group or a networking event. You may find common interest or even new interests with them, interests that will allow you to begin to move forward and create a new you.

Are you the kind of person who doesn't ask for help or has no answers when help is offered? Be kind to yourself. The emotions and changes going on inside your head can be overwhelming. A good practice is to sit down and make a list of what you need. Include needs for both tangible and emotional support. This could involve mowing the grass, grocery shopping, or simply talking on the phone when you need a supportive ear.

Get plenty of sleep and rest While you might not be able to sleep well while you are grieving, there are steps you can take to try to get a good night's rest and reestablish healthy sleep patterns. Establish bedtime rituals, such as reading a book or listening to a soothing song before bed. Avoid caffeine and alcohol in the evenings.

Writing Exercise:

When going through grief, so often we are afraid to ask for help, or we don't know what to ask from those offering. Take a stack of index cards and write down one of your needs or tasks on each card. When people ask how they can help, hand them a note card or have them choose something they feel they can do. This relieves the pressure to articulate your needs on the spot or to ask something of someone they are unwilling or unable to do.

_____

_____

_____

_____

_____

_____

Take care of yourself. In the days and weeks, maybe even months following your loved one's death, your physical routine might get disrupted. You may have trouble eating, sleeping, or participating in exercising.

Setting a goal of eating three meals daily, getting fresh air and exercise can work to be a diversion for you. Allow yourself to take some time away so that you can clear your head and can also help keep your mood elevated You can begin to remove yourself from certain situations by distancing yourself from things that remind you of the past.

Practicing ways to disconnect for a while will give you the chance to experience something positive -- even going to a local park without any access to social media.

Focus on your present and plan for your future. One of the most effective ways to let go of the past is to embrace the present. Instead of reliving the past and getting consumed with negativity, keep yourself active and enjoy the current moment.

Learn a new skill, meditate or exercise. Have dinner with a new friend or a supportive friend. Practice living in the present slowly and give yourself permission to leave your thoughts of the past in the past.

Begin to make new memories Start making new and positive memories to replace your sad memories from the past. Spend your time with the people who make you happy, doing things that bring you joy. Visit places that bring you peace.

Establish new patterns Memories and old ways of doing things can make it difficult to move on. Finding new ways does not mean that you are abandoning your loved one. Instead, it means that you are planning for your future.

Consider rearranging the furniture or doing some minor re-modeling. If you were used to watching television together, and now find you are unable to watch it, try inviting a friend to watch the program with you.

You are not forgetting your loved one, but are working towards allowing yourself to move on.

Returning to your favorite activities and work once the initial intense feelings of loss and pain have lessened can be beneficial in many ways. These activities will provide renewed friendship and companionship and will serve as a distraction from your pain and will allow you to get to a "new normal".

Maybe you are considering returning to work. It may be because you love your job, or you have to return to work for financial reasons. While the initial return might be difficult, getting back to your job will also allow you to think about the future instead of your past. It is possible that you will not have to return to full work duties right away.

Embrace new experiences If there is a place you've always wanted to visit or a hobby you always wanted to try, now might be a great time to try it. Although these new experiences won't eliminate your pain, they might allow you to meet new people and find new pathways to happiness.

Becoming Me After You

Part Five

"Grief is in two parts. The first is loss. The second is the remaking of life."

Anne Roiphe

Nurturing a "Newish" You

Challenge Five

Begin finding ways to develop your new self.

Engaging in public or private mourning rituals not only honors the deceased, but also allows the living to accept the loss.

Rituals of mourning often occur during a funeral or memorial service. Reciting a particular set of prayers or playing their favorite songs can allow friends and family time to share in their grief together. Participating in a mourning ritual can help start the healing process.

Once the formal services are over, it may help to develop a private mourning ritual for yourself.

Studies have shown that ongoing practices of these ritual behaviors can help a griever endure and flourish on with their life. There is no set timeframe for doing this. They can continue as long as you feel they bring you comfort.

Rituals can include prayers, meditation, or activities that bring comfort. Many times, they are unique to the mourner and their loved one.

They can be an important way to honor the memory of the deceased while allowing the living time to heal.

Judy shared that wearing her husband's sweater or another object owned by him whenever she felt sad was comforting.

Charles found going to the basketball court and sitting on his son's favorite bleacher once a week gave him time to silently think about him and talk to his son in heaven.

Listening to her husband's favorite album when she cooks a meal, Janice said, often bring tears to her eyes. Along with those tears, she also smiles as she remembers them listening to the songs together.

While caring for her mother, Cathy said they never forgot to say "good night" to each other every evening. It may have been in person with a warm hug, or over the telephone with one of them saying "I love you".

Now before Cathy turns out the lights she looks up, smiles and says good-night mom before bed each night.

Sharon confessed she has no rituals but agreed beginning some may help with her suffering.

As with many of the meetings, her fellow new-found friends offered her suggestions and support.

Judy suggested they talk it out. Speaking of talking things out, Sharon remembered they used to sit on the back porch and talk about everything. Charles told her he talked to his son often and this helped him. He suggested she try sitting out there and tell her how she is doing and ask him to bring her solace from her pain. She agreed to try it before they met again.

Sam shared that as long they had been together, they always said evening prayers before bed. Thanking the lord for the day and hoping their family and friends were blessed.

When the time came that Ruth could no longer recite hers or participate, he would sit next to her and do the prayers alone. Now that she is in Heaven, he continues to say those prayers believing she is saying them with him from above.

Preserve memories of your loved one. As time passes you might find that you can now begin to think of your loved one and feel happy instead of sadness or pain.

Embrace your feelings of joy and happiness, and think of all the gifts your loved one has provided for you.

Consider finding ways to preserve and honor the memory of your loved one's life. One way would be to create a memory book of events and photos of your loved one.

Ask friends and family members about their favorite experiences with your loved one and if they have pictures or clippings. Gather images, memories, and quotations together into a memory book.

When you are feeling particularly sad, you can read the memory book and remember the joy your loved one brought into the world for you and others.

When my sister died my mother took down every picture of her in the house. I know she was trying to spare herself the pain she felt.

That may work for some people, but I find I like looking at the pictures of my dad and my son and remembering the fun times.

We must try to remember that their death was not the defining moment of their life. The time they spent with you was much more important and valuable.

Think of the future. Above all, continue to move forward with your life and seek your own happiness. Your loved one would not want you to get stuck in a cycle of despair.

Grieve, but live your life. You can move into a bright and happy future and take the memories of your loved one with you.

Part of your own self-identity comes from the relationships you have with other people. When someone with whom you have a relationship dies, your self-identity, or the way you see yourself, naturally changes.

In some cases, you have to take on new roles, roles that had been filled by the person who died. After all, someone still has to take out the garbage, someone still has to buy the groceries and someone still has to balance the checkbook.

This can be very hard work and, at times, can leave you feeling drained of emotional, physical and spiritual energy. This is the time to begin to develop a new self-identity.

With the emergence of a new identity, you should also learn how to incorporate the part of who you are that was formed by the relationship you had with that person who is gone.

You may have once defined yourself as someone's son, daughter, father, mother, or friend. Since your loss, the way you define yourself and the way society defines you has also changed.

During the transformation you may discover some positive changes such as being more caring, less judgmental or being stronger than you once thought.

You may develop a renewed confidence in yourself. You may develop an assertive side of your identity that empowers you to keep going on and to thrive even though you still feel a sense of loss.

Reinventing or reconstructing your self-identity is long and hard work. It is important to remember that you have the right to move toward your grief, experience the pain and then begin the journey to heal.

Reconciling your grief will not happen quickly. Remember, grief is a process, not an event. Be patient and tolerant with yourself and avoid people who are impatient and intolerant with you. During this transformation your body, brain and spirit will begin to change.

Your Emotions:

When asked how the loss of a loved one and the group experience had changed her, Suzie replied, "I used to be quiet, reserved and accepting of others words and actions. Now that I have begun to learn how to speak up for myself, I feel more in control and have begun questioning other's demands of me. This has made me feel empowered."

Writing Exercise

I used to be __. Now that I have to _____, I am more ____. This makes me feel _____.

_____

_____

_____

_____

_____

_____

_____

Your Body:

If you were caring for someone who was ill, physical changes may have started long before the loss. You may have been spending hours, days, or even months ignoring your own self-care and focusing on their needs.

For some people following the death, self-care continues to not be a priority. They are consumed with focusing on their loss. They may not be eating balanced meals or skipping them altogether, and there may be changes in their sleeping habits. These actions can not only affect one's body, but can affect their emotions as well.

Your Emotional Heart:

Some days you may find you are more positive as you plan your future, but you will have days where it may feel like your heart has literally broken in two. On those days give yourself and your heart permission to grieve.

Allow yourself 10 to 15 minutes each day to acknowledge and feel your sadness. By giving it some dedicated attention without feeling guilty, you may find it popping up less often throughout your day.

Laughter can be a healing tool when working through your grief. Healing begins when one is able to look at the happy times and smile, to listen to a song and sing along rather than becoming tearful and to be able to one day laugh at a joke or funny movie.

There will be days the tears won't flow as hard or as often. A day will come when you will think of an event or special time when they made you laugh- and you will laugh again. You will be able to write a few memories of those times down and not become sad at their absence. A new you will begin to blossom

Your Mind:

The mind of bereaved people can remain stagnant as they try to hold onto their grief. For others, it can be the launching pad for new creative ideas and ways of life. Learning new skills through on-line classes or returning to school is one way to keep your mind focused and to grow intellectually and emotionally.

Begin to plan for the future and evaluate the choices you have made in the past and decide if they are still appropriate. Get out into the world again by teaching others something you are proficient in.

Become a friend to a newly grieving person or volunteer to help others.

Your Social Circle:

While you are traveling on your journey through grief, there were people who helped you and supported you in the past. Now that a new you is emerging, include them in your social activities. You may also want to try things you haven't done and make new friends. It's your ability now to begin to return to a "new normal" way of living.

One of the hardest things for Janice now that she is a single person, is to not feel like she is a "third wheel". Although her couple friends still invite her to dinner, she said she felt very lonely without her husband. She wished the wives would invite her to lunch while their husbands were at work. She thinks that may be an easier transition for her.

Your Spirituality:

You have the right to embrace your spirituality. If faith is a part of your life, express it in ways that seem appropriate to you. Allow yourself to be around people who understand and support your religious beliefs.

If you feel angry at God, find someone to talk with who won't be critical of your feelings of hurt and abandonment.

Questions regarding religion and faith will often surface during this time.

"How could God let this happen?" "Why did this happen now, and in this way?"

You might feel distant from your God or higher power, even questioning the very existence of God. You may feel rage and want to lash out at your God. Such feelings of doubt are normal.

Mourners often find themselves questioning their faith for months or even years before they rediscover the meaning in their life.

Be mindful of clichéd responses some people may give you. Comments like "It was God's will" or "Think of what you have to be thankful for". These comments are not helpful and you do not have to accept them.

Instead, helpful ways of self-emerging could be to create a sacred morning space, start each day with a meditation or prayer, organize a tree planting, visit the great outdoors.

For some grievers, it helps to imagine the person who died being up in heaven.

Janice said she finds it helpful to see her husband in heaven. He no longer is restrained with illness and had a wonderful reunion with his own parents and friends who had died previously.

Although they had completed writing assignments and shared them with the group, today was different. Today was just for themselves. She wanted them to begin looking at the changed person they had become. What did they want to do with this change? How could they now find purpose in their lives while bringing the memories and life experiences of their loved one?

Writing Exercise:

Make a list of what you want and what is wanted of you. Ask yourself "Who needs me now? Who depends on me? What am I good at that I can share with others? Ask yourself why were you put on this earth"? Make a list of these new goals:

_____

_____

_____

_____

_____

_____

_____

Part Six

"As long as we are mortal, death and grief will happen. Despite being in a painful experience, grieving is needed. Grieving is a natural way for us to learn to grow stronger and become more resilient. With guidance and support from others, our new self will begin to blossom and grow".

Mary Jane Cronin

Searching for Meaning

Challenge Six

Start searching for meaning in your past, present and future life

Searching for meaning and questioning what happened to the life you once knew is perfectly understandable. This however, also offers you the opportunity to begin investing in yourself and your future.

To do this means putting your emotional energy into new people and goals while still remembering your old world.

Begin establishing a new identity by creating a new relationship to the person who died.

Maybe there was a trait or talent you loved about them. Now is a good time to incorporate those traits into your new self.

Judy looked at the questions from the previous chapter and started talking. "I had been caring for my husband for so long, I don't know who needs me and depends on me now? I don't feel I have a purpose anymore."

Mary asked her what she had learned while caring for husband about his care needs? Could she help a wife whose husband was recently diagnosed with Parkinson's? What could she advise her about self-care and avoiding caregiver burnout?

Could she take the memory of the beauty of her husband's paintings and begin taking photographs of nature herself?

Everyone is good at something. The trick is to look past today and rediscover something you love and can share with others.

Writing Exercise:

Today Mary asked them to do something called "free-writing". This is when you write fast what is on your mind without thinking about it first. She asked them to write about these questions Why did you have to experience this loss when others never feel such pain? What can you share with others as a result of your loss?

_____

_____

_____

_____

_____

As she waited for the group members to finish their answers, Mary shared her answer with the group. "It took time for me to realize I had to experience my loss so I could help others. I had to go through my own grief, feel my own pain, and reach the other side to tell others it was possible". My life with my son, his death, and my life since that day has changed me. It has allowed me to bring a part of him into my present and future since that terrible day."

Dottie asked if she could share even though she didn't have to. She said she had reflected on why she had experienced this loss at this time. She said she had positive memories of life with her mother. She realized she wanted the same relationship with her daughter and could do things to ensure that happening. She had become more involved in her daughter's life and was working on keeping communications between them open.

When someone you love dies, you naturally question the meaning and purpose of life. What are some of the "why" questions that have come up for you since the death? Go through those questions with a friend or counselor who won't feel she has to give you all the answers. Some of your questions may have answers, but some may not.

Reconciliation versus Resolution.

Reconciliation focuses on the relationship and resolution focuses on the problem. There will never be a resolution or end to your grief. We never truly get over our loss, and life will never turn back to the normal as we knew it. We will instead, change and grow within ourselves and learn a new way of living.

The goal is to instead find reconciliation to our loss.

The dictionary defines reconciliation as "the process of making two people or groups of people friendly again after being kept apart from each other".

When we take the definition and relate it to the loss of a loved one, we are now entwining the living being we once knew and the memories and love of that being with each other.

When we begin the integration process, we are slowly moving forward in the emotional concept of our loved one being with us without their physical presence. A renewed energy and confidence are soon discovered. The goal is finding a way to fully acknowledge the death, while finding the capacity to become involved in the activities of living.

It is the act of changing the relationship with the person from someone who died, to one of memory and the beginning of learning and redirecting of their energy.

Receiving ongoing support from others is crucial in our success and discovery of our new life. We need to receive ongoing support from others. Not only do we need the love and understanding of others immediately following our loss, we may need it for years to come.

Remember that grief is a process, not an event, and you will need support for weeks, months and maybe even years.

Drawing on the experience and encouragement of friends, fellow grievers or professional counselors is not a weakness but a healthy human need. The quality and amount of understanding support you get during your work of mourning will have a major influence on your capacity to heal and flourish.

To be truly helpful, the people in your support system must appreciate the impact this death has had on you. They must understand that in order to heal, you must be allowed – even encouraged – to mourn long after the death and if needing it, learn to become re-born yourself.

During the transition, friends must encourage you to see mourning not as an enemy to be overcome, but something to be experienced as a result of having loved someone.

Your inner resources and surrounding support system will both play a role in your healing during your grief journey. It is through discovering your sense of self, where you are now in the grief process and will be in the future of your healing process. This also comes from the people close to you who have shared on this journey with you.

"Growing within" means allowing those changes to happen. This happens by talking with others, writing in journals, or seeing it in your mind, and then taking action to make it happen.

Signs that our loved ones are near

Some say that seeing signs of their loved ones is a way of blending the past with the present. Others say it is all in the mind of the survivor. In speaking with people for the book I asked them if they saw signs and what did they think it meant?

The top signs mentioned by the group were finding pennies, seeing cardinals, hearing music and smells that reminded them of their loved one, and butterflies.

Cathy said she was always finding pennies and dines. Never nickels or quarters, she laughed. Pennies from Heaven are said to signify a new chapter or fresh start. Some people say they are being left from the angel of a loved one bringing us comfort and love and let us know we are not alone.

Janice said when she lived up north, she saw cardinals a few times after someone died. She had heard when you see a cardinal an angel is nearby.

Known to be the most notable spirit messenger, they often remind one that their loved one is watching and over them.

Sharon reminded everyone how music played a big role in their relationship. She said she hears songs they listened to whenever she is near a place they went to. Other people, including myself, believe in their loved one sending them music. Driving to the cemetery the radio would often play one of Jeremy's favorite songs. Those songs would bring tears and smiles as I picture him singing with me from Heaven.

Janice said it may seem strange, but sometimes I think I can smell the aroma of Frank's pipe smoke. I was surprised that a few members of the group said they had smelled a familiar scent such as perfume or cigarette. Researchers have discovered that our sense of smell is linked to our memory recall abilities. The smells could indeed mean a loved one is in your presence.

Charles shared he believed in the butterfly sending a "hello dad" greeting from his son. Butterflies represent change and growth.

For Charles, watching a butterfly emerging from a cocoon, he saw Tommy's journey to heaven and the changes and potential growth taking place in his own life.

The Final Session:

At the last gathering of the group Mary asked them what had changed in their lives since joining the group? "Who would like to share what they have learned about themselves and their ability to give to others during our sessions together"?

Cathy shared that she had always made flower boxes for her mom for Mother's Day. After she died, Cathy had a stone engraved that says, 'Remembering Mom in her Garden.' "It helps me hold precious memories."

During her time visiting and caring for her mother she had become friends with other residents and their families. She had been visiting after her mother passed to visit with them. She took a class and became a volunteer at the facility. Sometimes they shared stories about her mom but other times they talked about their own care journey or families.

Charles said he had started a men's group at his church. He said had begun talking with other fathers who had lost their own children.

Being an all men made the group focus on different topics than the ones in this group. Charles admitted what he learned from our group had prepared him to start his own group. He said that men think they need to hold things inside, to appear strong. Talking about his loss and how it made him feel in both groups was helping himself as well as the fellow fathers.

During one of his church's' meetings, he was told about an organization called Open to Hope. Doing some research, he found out in addition to the many services, they offered on-line support for people who had lost their loved ones including their children. He contacted them, found they accepted stories from parents about their loss and what they had learned from the loss. Not only was his letter accepted. he now was a contributing writer with the program.

Many people see beauty and symbolism in a butterfly release to honor their child. Charles learned how to conduct one of his own in his town and plans to continue it annually in honor of Tommy.

One of Judy's friends belonged to a women's group that did volunteer work in the community. She, too, had lost her husband and found the work and comradery of the women helped her find a new purpose.

Judy donated some of her husband's paintings to the meeting hall and felt he was with her and smiling down whenever she attended a meeting.

Contacting them, Judy was able to become a permanent part of the organization as well. When they met to discuss a fundraiser, Judy thought of all the beautiful paintings Bob had created and the horrible illness that took him away from her.

Volunteering and raising money for research was a great way for her to carry on his memory and help raise funds for a cure.

The group had decided to dedicate an event in his memory. Judy found her heart feeling full as the event was created showing times of their life and the hope of inspiring others to follow their passion.

Dottie wanted everyone to know the group had helped strengthen the relationship with her daughter. They had begun talking more about her mom, expressing their feelings about how each one felt. She realized that she had the power to make the future what she wanted. To learn from the past but not stay there.

Sam, who was experienced in advanced directives, had completed he and Ruth's early in their marriage. He understood that when a person with dementia reaches a certain mental limitation, advanced directives can no longer be signed. He found doing this early gave families piece of mind. Following the end of the group sessions, he began working with another lawyer offering free sessions for dementia patients and their families. He said it was rewarding to help them in memory of Ruth.

One other thing Sam decided to do was start a program to send someone to college. He contacted the local high school to establish an educational scholarship in accounting for local a student.

Sharon decided to advance herself in honor of Roy and complete what he couldn't. She enrolled in night school to earn her GED diploma and go to college for counseling. She hoped to learn more about suicide and addiction to help prevent others from experiencing her pain.

Finishing something that meant a lot to your loved one is a way to honor their contribution to the world and to connect to their sense of purpose.

Suzie became a volunteer at the dog rescue facility on weekends. Rather than replace Chico until she was emotionally ready, she was able to foster a few puppies herself while the paperwork was being filled out for their new forever home.

Janice said she had returned to her church and discovered they had a chapter of Women of Hope. This is a non-profit organization that helps widows learn skills, find support and make friends. They meet for lunch and fellowship, have community outings, and one-on one support for women.

Janice said she had begun to make pillows for her sons out of their dad's shirts. "I also had a pillow made for myself, using his favorite shirt. I keep it on my bed next to that blanket that even now still smells like Frank."

Finding that she enjoyed it so much and it brought her comfort, she had started offering services to others who had lost someone.

So far she had made quilts for three sisters out of their father's flannel shirts with each quilt having a picture of them with their dad."

All eight of the group members found they smiled more and cried less. Agreeing that the goal of the group was met, finding a way to remember their loved one and embracing the hope for the future.

They ended the evening by hugging good-bye and promising to keep in contact with each other through phone calls or meetings. They all agreed that they now understood the benefit of having support from others who have walked the journey of loss themselves.

In closing:

The loss of a significant person in our lives can be an intense experience. Allow yourself to feel and experience your sadness in your own way. Remember your reaction to the loss is yours alone. Give yourself time to feel your emotions and hold onto your memories and your special relationship with the deceased.

You will know when you feel emotionally ready to begin practicing self-care that allows you to begin healing while still honoring your loved one.

Look for ways to honor your life together while learning to discover your new identity.

Give yourself permission to grow and change into the role you now have; this gives you the opportunity to live and share with others.

Create ways to keep your loved one in your heart life as you see best suited to you. Maybe having pictures hanging in the home, maybe plant a garden of their favorite flowers, or if they loved a sport such as fishing, sit by the lake and picture them smiling down on you.

"When those you love die, the best you can do is honor their spirit for as long as you live. You make a commitment that you're going to take whatever lesson that person or animal was trying to teach you, and you make it true in your own life. It's a positive way to keep their spirit alive in the world by keeping it alive in yourself."

Patrick Swayze

Becoming Me After You

Resources

Twenty years of being a licensed counselor and helping people work through their losses has resulted in my gathering valuable and useful information. I have had the opportunity of meeting and learning from fellow authors specializing in loss and grief.

Attending seminars, presenting at conventions and having conversations with many of the speakers provided me with much of the material in this book.

Working at Suncoast Hospice for ten years and enrolling in their bereavement program enabled me to help the patients admitted to accept and adjust to their diagnosis. And, to help their family members grieve, remember and grow with loving memories in their heart.

About the Author

Mary Jane Cronin has over 20 years of experience counseling individuals and groups dealing with grief and loss, work life balance, caregiving, stress and unexpected changes in their lives. A native of New Jersey, she left the Jersey Shores for the Florida beaches and has lived in the Tampa Bay area for over 40 years.

Mary enjoys speaking privately to one person or to a group about self-care needs when dealing with changes in a family or work life. She lectures and has taught support skills to teenagers, incarcerated women, hospice patients and their families, as well as to hospice volunteers, and fellow health care professionals.

Her passion to help people reclaim the emotional balance in their lives motivated her to publish her books, Becoming Me After You is Mary Jane's seventh book. Her writing career began following the death of her son, when she wrote and published November Mourning. Mary Jane, a licensed mental health counselor, earned her Bachelor's Degree in Human Development from Eckerd College in St Petersburg, Florida, and her Master's Degree in Community Psychology from Springfield College in Springfield, Massachusetts.

Ms. Cronin was employed in the health care field for ten years. Following her departure, she opened her private practice where she offers counseling, coaching, and professional speaking.

CONNECT WITH MARY JANE ON SOCIAL MEDIA

https://twitter.com/CounselorMary

https://www.facebook.com/maryjanecronin1

linkedin.com/in/mary-jane-cronin-63a957101

https://www.youtube.com/channel/UCAoAhii58HkCx2u4sZzx7QQ

Other Books by Mary Jane Cronin

November Mourning Mary Jane Cronin has written not just a fact- filled book about loss and grief, but one that included her personal journey to understand, accept and heal following the 1998 murder of her own son. November Mourning offers insight and hope as it explores the emotions parents feel following the loss of a child. Travel with Mary Jane through the stages of grief and develop techniques to help move through them easier. Discover what other parents have said and done to help reduce their own suffering. ISBN: 978-0615239781

Writing Through Your Grief Writing Through your Grief is a guidebook to help you through a loss. Losing someone you love is difficult. Trying to continue in a world without them is even more difficult. Writing Through your Grief offers you an opportunity to reflect on your time together, your emotions and the way you have dealt with grief in the past. Through the writing prompts, you will share stories, and learn about the healing process.

Although you will never be "over" it, it is my hope you will one day be able to smile when you share stories about them ... rather than fill with tears. ISBN: 978-0984501601

A Caregiver's Connection We are living longer these days. The result is often a loved one faced with illness and limitations requiring a caregiver to step in and help with their care. Many wives, daughters, even sons and husbands are also taking on this role with little or no training and knowledge of what to do. A Caregiver's Connection offers resources, and self-care ideas for the caregivers. ISBN: 978-0984501625

Unexpected Change We often fear change, resist it, and even try to avoid it from happening. We begin to accept change when we have control of it. In this book you will learn there are several factors that determine our response to inevitable changes and what you can do to be able to accept and adapt to change. ISBN: 9780984501632

Growing Through Illness Together When someone you love is diagnosed with a terminal illness or disease there are many unanswered questions. Growing Through Illness Together is an informative yet personal guide of what to expect. Filled with medical facts with just enough personal stories it helps the reader understand the steps that happen not only to the person diagnosed, but also to the caregiver, spouse, and loved ones. The tips and advice given on how to move forward is inspiring and comforting. ISBN: 978-0-9845016

Tied in Knots: 3 Steps to Releasing Stress. When asked if they would like to reduce their stress the majority of people would raise up their hands saying "Yes!"

In your past, you may have been conditioned to accept stress as a part of life, but this doesn't have to be your future fate. With Tied in Knots you will be able to reduce stress in five minutes or less with practical exercises and develop strategies for you. ISBN: 978-0-9845016-6-3

Additional copies and other books may be ordered at www.maryjanecronin.com